Smelly
Old History
Reeking Royals

Mary Dobson

OXFORD UNIVERSITY PRESS

Oxford University Press, Great Clarendon Street, Oxford OX2 6DP

Oxford New York
Athens Auckland Bangkok Bogotá Buenos Aires Calcutta
Cape Town Chennai Dar es Salaam Delhi Florence Hong Kong Istanbul
Karachi Kuala Lumpur Madrid Melbourne Mexico City Mumbai
Nairobi Paris São Paulo Singapore Taipei Tokyo Toronto Warsaw
and associated companies in Berlin Ibadan

Oxford is a registered trade mark of Oxford University Press

Published in the United States
by Oxford University Press Inc., New York

© Mary Dobson 1998
The moral rights of the author have been asserted
First published 1998

Artwork: Vince Reid. Photographs reproduced by kind permission of:
p.16 The Board of Trustees of the Armouries, XV.1 and XV.3; p.18
British Museum; p.29 Crown copyright, Historic Royal Palaces.

British Library Cataloguing in Publication Data available

ISBN   0 19 910529 4

1 3 5 7 9 10 8 6 4 2

Printed in Great Britain

CONTENTS

Scratch the scented panels lightly with a fingernail
to release their smell.

A SENSE OF THE PAST

Imagine being a famous king or queen. Just think of all that power and wealth! Your outer layers, alone, might be worth a small fortune. With a great golden crown on your anointed head, fingers dripping with jewels, layers of scented robes, and a thick padded throne for your tender seat, you can rule the world. But beware! Outward trappings can be deceptive. Some kings and queens of the past weren't quite so nice underneath. And some were positively revolting.

Of all the senses of the past, the smells are often forgotten. It's probably just as well when it comes to the *Reeking Royals*. This book gives you a fresh (and not so fresh) view of royal history.

Since ancient times, many countries have been ruled by a royal family. The firstborn son was usually heir to the throne. Some royals went to great lengths to produce a boy. Bloody battles were fought over kingdoms. Many monarchs had nasty ends, bumped off by their rotten subjects, or murdered by their rivals. All in all, royals have had a pretty foul time. It's not surprising many of them stank to high heaven!

It's said that James I never had a bath in his life! While onlookers sniffed, James scratched! He had special slits in his dagger-proof doublet so he could poke his fleas.

Henry VIII had some odorous habits. His loyal courtier, the Groom of the Stool, is not going to risk his head by complaining.

Marie Antoinette, queen of France, was guillotined by her revolting subjects in 1793.

Reeking Royals

Kings and queens had all the luck,
With pots of loot and not much muck....
Well, that's the history you've been told,
But wait to smell the truth unfold.

The royals in this stinky book
Are really not the way they look.
Their pretty little velvet thrones
Smelled just as foul as old fish bones.

They gorged themselves on rotten meals,
And stuffed their tums with slimy eels.
They fought like mad in fields of mud
And stank of filth and sweat and blood.

A few, of course, were fresh and sweet
And sloshed strong scents on face and feet.
Too bad some fragrant kings and queens
Had heads chopped off by guillotines.

At home these royals had lots and lots
Of servants to clean their chamber pots.
But don't forget, if you were loyal
You wouldn't dare say 'Reeking Royal'.

AROMATIC ANCIENTS

The reeking royals of ancient civilizations soon found a way to disguise their rotten smells — they smeared their bodies, clothes and hair with thick layers of perfume.

In this splendid scene, Egyptian ships in 1600 BC are loading up with stacks of myrrh, ebony, incense and gold in the land of Punt, far to the south of Egypt. These exotic goods are for Queen Hatshepsut of the Egyptian New Kingdom. The queen adores wonderful fragrances and fills her temple at Der-el-Bahari with the strongest scents. There's enough here to overpower a whole kingdom.

Queen Hatshepsut

Nebuchadnezzar II, king of Babylon, built the most wonderful hanging gardens in 600 BC. They were filled with every kind of fragrant tree that you can imagine.

But not all ancients were quite so aromatic. Miserable Moquihuixtli, Mexican ruler of Tlatelolco, sent his wife packing because he found her breath so unbearable. The queen's brother thought this was most unfair. He declared war and killed the king.

Scratch and sniff for a terrible whiff of the queen's beastly breath.

REVOLTING ROMANS

Ancient Roman rulers could be really revolting. They overpowered each other with perfumes — and poisons. In 509 BC the Romans did away with their conspiring kings. Five centuries later, they had a great big empire ruled by emperors who employed slaves to freshen up their stinks. They used giant syringes to spray perfumes everywhere.

Romulus and Remus were twin brothers who were brought up from babies by a she-wolf. Romulus founded Rome, murdered Remus and set the trend for the rest of the reeking Romans.

Augustus, the first Roman emperor, ate a fig lovingly poisoned by his wife Livia.

Cccc...claudius stuttered and stumbled his way through Rome. His enemies tried to poison him with mouldy mushrooms, which gave him the runs. Eventually, his doctor, Xenophon, finished him off by tickling his throat with a deadly feather.

Cruel Caligula expected everyone to worship him as a god — even his perfumed horse. After he was stabbed, his enemies took their revenge by tasting his flesh!

Nero, emperor of Rome from AD 37 to 68, was quite disgusting. He put on spectacular shows such as this one, drenching everyone in sight with scents and blood. Here he is preparing to kill human victims. In the end, Nero murdered almost every member of his family and then killed himself.

Medieval monarchs rarely took baths (apart from King John).

Henry I couldn't resist eating eels. Sadly they proved to be the end of him.

MOULDY MONARCHS

Many medieval monarchs gave the royals a rotten reputation. They were forever fighting. They gorged themselves on huge banquets and suffered from foul diseases. Still, some of them came to a grisly end.

William the Conqueror popped over to England in 1066, from Normandy in France, and killed his rival King Harold at the Battle of Hastings. Having conquered England, he built the Tower of London, which became a pungent prison for many future reeking royals.

William, himself, had a mouldy end. In 1087, he wanted to get his own back on the French for making rude comments about his waistline. In the battle, William's horse stumbled. He fell on to the pommel of his saddle and ruptured his intestines.

At William's funeral, his bloated tummy burst as it was stuffed into the tomb. It created the most revolting stench, which quickly overcame the French.

Scratch and sniff for a deadly whiff.

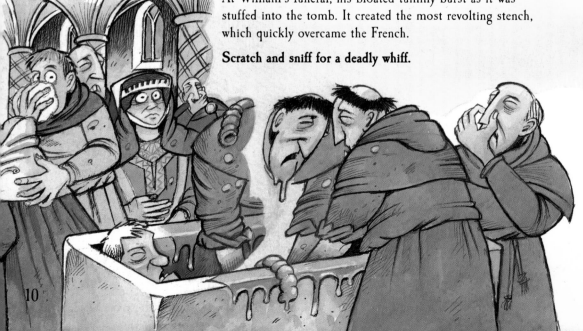

Richard III was the last English king to die on the battlefield. He was slain at the Battle of Bosworth against Henry Tudor in 1485. His body was stripped naked, slung over a horse and taken to Leicester to be buried — a smelly spectacle for the sniggering crowds.

Henry VI was murdered in the Tower of London in 1471.

SCENTED SOVEREIGNS

The lands of Africa, Arabia and Asia were often ruled by spicy sultans and fruity sultanas (sultans' wives!), scented shahs and exotic emperors oozing with oils. They lived in perfumed palaces, with gorgeous gardens and breathtaking beasts.

A scented sultan and his sultana wallow in the Turkish bath. Too long in here and she will end up all wrinkly! A spicy feast awaits them.

Shah Jahan, ruler of the Mogul empire in India in the 17th century, sits on his jewelled Peacock Throne.

But life for the scented sovereigns of the East wasn't always so sweet. They were hungry for power. Famous royal warriors, like Genghis Khan (the Mongolian leader), Suleiman the Magnificent (sultan of the Ottoman Empire), Babur and Akbar (Mogul emperors, who ruled India) fought many bloody battles to extend their empires and defend their religious beliefs.

Tamerlane, the merciless Mongol emperor of the 14th century, made towers from the heads of his enemies outside the walls of cities he wished to frighten into surrender— not a pretty sight. As the heads rotted, they gave off a foul stench and a ghostly light.

When Saladin, the Muslim sultan, captured Jerusalem in AD 1187 after defeating the crusaders, he had the great mosque scrubbed with gallons of rosewater to make it fit for prayer.

LOVE AND LAVENDER

Catherine of Aragon: divorced

Anne Boleyn: beheaded

Jane Seymour: died

Anne of Cleves: divorced

Catherine Howard: beheaded

Catherine Parr: survived

The odorous Tudors loved delicious smells and spices. Everything in their royal palaces in the 16th century was drenched in lavender — slippers, gloves, armpits. Even the pets were scented! But behind the scenes, things weren't quite so fragrant.

Henry VIII had three passions — perfumes, food and ladies! He quickly got a foul reputation — for chopping and changing his wives. He had six in total, and only Jane Seymour produced a male heir for him.

By the time he was 50 years old, Henry had a waistline of 135 cm (54 inches) and had to be hoisted in and out of his 4-metre-wide bed by pulleys and ropes. Three huge people could get inside his doublet. (Not that you'd want to — phew!)

Here Henry is thrilled with the birth of his son. Edward, however, was a sickly lad. After his dad's death in 1547 the young king ruled for only six years before snuffing it.

Scratch and sniff for a lovely whiff of the royal bedchamber.

Lady Jane Grey slipped in next.
She holds the record for being
the shortest reigning British
monarch — nine days. In typical
fashion, she was axed by the next
royal — her cousin Mary.

Mary I ordered the burning of nearly 300
Protestants at the stake, and was nicknamed
Bloody Mary. She married Philip II of Spain,
who is said to have been offended by her
sickly smell.

Henry VIII's daughter, Elizabeth I, never married
but she reigned a good long time (1558—1603).
She once said: 'I know I have but the body of a
weak and feeble woman, but I have the heart and
stomach of a king'. Fortunately, she didn't have her
dad's stomach and she wasn't quite as heartless!

FOUL FASHIONS

Some royal fashions caught on really quickly — others didn't last. Some royal habits changed the course of history.

Terrible tortures
Henry VIII ordered the execution of over 50,000 of his revolting subjects.

Count Vlad Dracul ruled the small country of Wallachia from 1456 to 1476. He didn't suck blood but, apparently, he liked to watch his victims being impaled on spikes while he savoured his supper. The smell was said to be unbearable. He became known as Vlad the Impaler.

Hairy ordeals
The pharaohs of Egypt wore false beards tied on with string to make them look old and wise. Even the queens wore beards.

Elizabeth I had 80 perfumed wigs to cover up her bald head. Charles II began to wear a wig in 1666 when he started going grey. Wigs soon became the height of fashion!

Touchy subjects

Some monarchs believed they could cure their subjects of a disease called scrofula, or the King's Evil, by a divine touch. Charles II 'touched' nearly 100,000 subjects. In one year seven people were crushed to death trying to get near him.

The bloodstained shirt and underpants worn by Charles I at his execution were hung up in a London church for 'touching' until 1860.

Potty ideas

Egyptian royals bathed in fresh blood to give them superior strength.

19th century-Prince Christian of Schleswig-Holstein lost an eye and used a variety of glass ones. His best one was a bloodshot eye which he wore when he had a cold.

FATAL FUMES

Many royals were plagued by the foul smells around them. From ancient times, they fumigated their palaces with strong scents to overcome disease and evil.

The idea took a fatal twist in the 17th century when the smelly Stuarts tried out the latest craze from America — tobacco smoke to 'freshen' the air. During the terrible plague epidemic of 1665 the King's Scholars at Eton College (founded by Henry VI in 1440) were beaten if they were caught NOT smoking!

Incense, such as myrrh and frankincense, was burned in special holders at all Egyptian religious ceremonies.

But James I described smoking as 'a custom loathsome to the eye, hateful to the nose, harmful to the brain, and dangerous to the lung'. He wrote a book called *Counterblast to Tobacco* — the first anti-smoking campaign!

In the 19th century, the royals tried to snuff out fatal diseases like cholera by burning bonfires in the cities. This fuming solution failed miserably. From 1837 to 1901 Queen Victoria reigned over the largest empire in the world, but she couldn't find a fresh solution for her 53 overflowing cesspools at Windsor Castle. Young Winston Churchill was not amused: 'I can see little glory in an empire which can rule the waves and is unable to flush the sewers.'

PERFUMED PARISIANS

Frenchkings and queens of the 17th century were famous for their extravagant clothes and perfumes. Their royal bodies dripped with luscious scents and luxurious silks. Unfortunately, by the end of the 18th century their heads dripped with a less pleasant odour, as they were hacked off by the guillotine.

Louis XIV (1643-1715) holds the record as the longest reigning monarch in the world. Known as the Sun King because he dazzled like the sun, he was said to be the 'sweetest-smelling' royal ever. He wore a different perfume every day.

In 1661 Louis built a brilliant palace at Versailles, near Paris. It has a total of 264 close stools for his royal visits. Louis XIV is so fond of these 'thrones', he even receives his guests while sitting at ease.

Servants perfume Louis XIV's rooms with rose water and marjoram.

They wash his shirts in a stew of cloves, nutmeg, aloe, jasmine, orange water and musk.

The king is so wrapped up in his own fragrance he hasn't noticed the disgusting smells around him. The thousands of courtiers, servants and messengers who come to the palace each day to attend his every whim have to make do with any old corner!

The courtiers squabble jealously to become holder of the royal left sock, or remover of the royal underpants.

After a while, Parisian visitors complain that this splendid palace reeks of lavatories. This doesn't worry Louis XVI (1754-1793) and his wife Marie Antoinette. They like strong scents! But the French peasants find these reeking royals too overpowering. In 1793, the revolting French haul the king and queen off to the guillotine and do away with their monarchy.

When the royals returned to Versailles in the 19th century, the smell of urine and excrement still lingered!

SMELLY SERVICE

If you weren't born lucky (or unlucky) enough to be a reeking royal, you could always give a helping hand in one of these juicy jobs.

Convenient courtiers
These ladies-in-waiting aren't potty. They know poor pregnant Anne Boleyn can't wait to get through her coronation.

These 14th-century Chinese courtiers aren't quite so wiped out by royal events. Their emperor is using the first sheets of royal loo paper in the world. It's soft and perfumed.

Model workers
Egyptian pharaohs had a different servant for each bit of their body. Imagine being caretaker of the royal toenails!

Taharqo, a Kushite king (in Nubia), hoped for a cushy after-life. He took 1070 model workers, or shabtis, with him to the grave in 664 BC.

The kings and queens of ancient Sumeria had their living servants buried with them — they soon stopped working inside the deadly tomb.

Royal ratcatchers

Not surprisingly, royals haven't been too keen on stinking rats and bugs in their bed. Queen Victoria kept a royal ratcatcher and bug-destroyer to do her dirty work.

Hairy dressers

With so many clothes, wigs and fiddly bits, royals needed a lot of help dressing and undressing. Elizabeth I owned 3000 garments. These were too heavy to wash, so they were perfumed instead. Keeping her smelling fresh must have been fun.

Palace perfumers

Darius III, king of Persia, had 14 full-time perfumers and 46 garland-makers.

Alexander the Great ordered his servants to perfume the floors of his royal apartments and soak his tunics in scent.

Cleopatra kept her perfumers on their toes — when Mark Antony popped in for a little snack, she had her banqueting hall filled knee-deep with roses.

GROANS AND GASES

Queasy queens and kings suffered from stomach upsets, caused by foul diseases or rotten food. To make matters worse, they were dosed with nasty medicines to help release their ghastly gases. Royal physicians in the past had no idea what was wrong with their patients, or what cures to use — and they often lost their patience trying to treat them.

Poor old King George III (1760-1820) suffered terribly from his gassy disorders (wind!). He suffered even more once the doctors got their hands on him. When his urine turned strange colours, his despairing doctors went completely mad. They put burning hot cups on his skin to get rid of his bad odours. Sadly, this didn't work. Now we know that George and other royals suffered from an inherited disease called porphyria.

Poor George was accused of doing crazy things like talking to trees — he thought an oak tree was his royal friend, Frederick the Great.

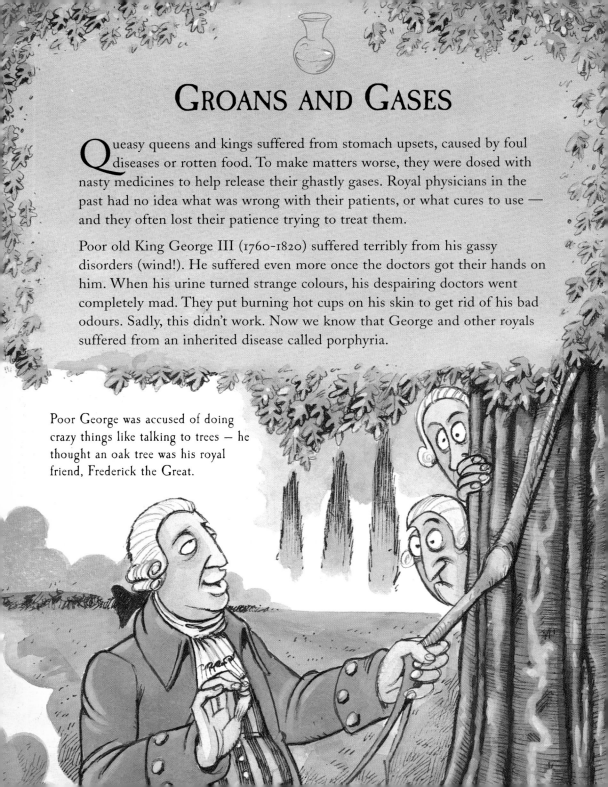

The Royal Wee

King George the Third smelt very bad.
His loyal realm declared him mad.
The royal wee had turned to blue
And King George knew not what to do.
He talked and talked a lot of rot
And passed around his foul piss-pot.

His doctors were all bumbling fools.
They felt his pulse and smelled his stools.
They put hot cups upon his legs
To draw out all his smelly dregs.
The king cried out with so much pain,
'This cupping lark is all in vain'.

No end of cures they tried to find
To see if they could change his mind.
'Twas all no good, his craze got worse,
Blue urine was a right royal curse.
Since those mad days, we have found out
Just what blue wee is all about.

George had a gene that made his bottom
Hurt and smell something quite rotten.
Porphyria was the real name
Of poor King George's maddening shame.
We always thought royal blood was blue,
But now we know royal wee was too!

NASTY ENDS

Few royals were lucky enough to die peacefully in bed. Kings and queens — both cruel and kind — have had foul ends. Some had their lives chopped short and some lost their heads.

Caught short
Edmund Ironside, son of Elthelred the Unready, had a surprise attack when he was murdered in his privy in 1016. His enemy hid in the cesspit before taking the plunge.

Exploding monarchs
George IV's corpse had a lucky escape. As he was lying in state in a lead coffin, his decomposing body began to swell. To stop it exploding, his attendants punctured the coffin to let out the gas!

Heads down
Anne Boleyn (1536), Mary Queen of Scots (1587), Charles I (1649) and Louis XVI (1793) were all given the chop. Anne's lips were said to be moving after her head was cut off. The head of Mary Queen of Scots was chopped three times before it came off. When the executioner eventually lifted the head off the block, it fell on to the floor. He was left just holding her wig.

Bottoms up

Edward II (1307-1327) had a truly terrible end. He was imprisoned in Berkeley Castle. His traitors, spurred on by his wife, Isabella, had to find a way to kill him without leaving a mark. A red hot poker was the end result.

Stinky cover-ups

Shih Huang Ti's death in 210 BC was carefully covered up — foul fish were placed in his carriage so nobody would notice the smell of his decaying corpse!

Scratch and sniff for a rotten fishy whiff

When Queen Anne was dying in 1714, her doctors tried everything — even massaging her feet with garlic!

Last of a line

Montezuma, the Aztec emperor, and Atahualpa, king of the Incas in the 16th century, were both killed by invading Spanish conquistadores (conquerors). The Aztec and Inca civilizations collapsed completely after their deaths.

In 1918, revolting Russian rebels shot Tsar Nicholas II and his family. It was a rotten end for the Russian royals.

CROWNING GLORIES

Life for the royals hasn't always been quite so nasty. Some kings, queens and emperors had glorious starts and fragrant farewells. Imagine wearing a crown of feathers on your head ... or ending up in a tomb full of goodies.

The coronation of this Egyptian pharaoh is a sumptuous spicy event.

Aztec and Inca emperors wore tickly topknots like this feather headdress.

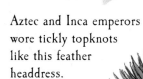

The crowning glory of this Yoruba king is this beaded headgear.

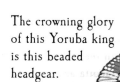

Since Charles I, British monarchs have been anointed with a special holy oil which smells heavenly.

King John lost his Crown jewels in the Wash in 1216 — they may still be there! Four centuries later, Colonel Blood tried to steal the new jewels, but his pursuers were hot on his scent. The precious jewels are now on display (under lock and key) in the Tower of London.

This African king was dressed for the occasion -- he was popped into his tomb in full royal regalia and seated upright on a throne.

This richly perfumed Chinese prince, Liu Sheng, and his princess were buried in elaborate jade suits in 113 BC. They took with them to the afterlife six carriages, 16 horses, 11 dogs and enough food and drink for a lifetime. They even had a bathroom in their tomb! Unfortunately, when the tomb was opened their suits had shattered and their bodies looked a bit jaded.

Shih Huang Ti, the first Chinese emperor in the 3rd century BC, had an entire terracotta army of 10,000 life-size model soldiers, to protect his reeking tomb.

PUNGENT PUZZLES

Heads and tails

Try and fit these heads to their rightful royal owners.

Noble and noxious

Pair up these names for a round-up of reeking royals:

IVAN	THE MAGNIFICENT
ETHELRED	THE TERRIBLE
ALFRED	THE IMPALER
SULEIMAN	THE LIONHEART
VLAD	THE GREAT
RICHARD	THE UNREADY

GLOSSARY

cholera	a disease caused by germs in water or food
close stool	a chair or stool with a built-in chamber pot, used as a toilet
coronation	a ceremony for crowning a monarch
fumigate	to use smoke or fumes to get rid of bad smells and vermin
guillotine	a machine for slicing off a person's head
heir	someone who inherits something, for example the role of monarch
incense	a substance that makes a spicy smell when it is burned
jade	a pale green stone
myrrh	a substance used in perfumes and incense
pommel	the raised part of a horse's saddle
porphyria	a disease that is inherited
revolution	a rebellion that overthrows the government
scrofula	a disease that affects the neck
shabti	an Egyptian model which was buried in tombs, to work for the dead person
shah	a monarch of certain lands, especially in the Middle East
sultan, sultana	the male and female rulers of certain Muslim countries

31

INDEX